CARDBOARD CREATURE CHALLENGE!

Joanne Mattern

DiscoverRoo
An Imprint of Pop!
popbooksonline.com

abdobooks.com

Published by Pop!, a division of ABDO, PO Box 398166, Minneapolis, Minnesota 55439. Copyright © 2021 by POP, LLC. International copyrights reserved in all countries. No part of this book may be reproduced in any form without written permission from the publisher. Pop!™ is a trademark and logo of POP, LLC.

Printed in the United States of America, North Mankato, Minnesota.

052020
092020

♻ **THIS BOOK CONTAINS RECYCLED MATERIALS**

Cover Photos: Red Line Editorial, top left; Shutterstock Images, top right, bottom
Interior Photos: Red Line Editorial, 1 (top left), 21, 23 (top), 26, 28, 29; Shutterstock Images, 1 (top right), 1 (bottom), 14, 19 (top), 27; iStockphoto, 5, 6, 7, 8, 9, 11, 12, 13, 15, 17, 20, 23 (bottom), 25, 30, 31; Juan Garcia Aunión/agefotostock/Alamy, 18; Ekaterina Demidova/Alamy, 19 (bottom); Anan Kaewkhammul/Alamy, 22 (top), 22 (bottom)

Editor: Meg Gaertner
Series Designer: Jake Slavik

Library of Congress Control Number: 2019955013

Publisher's Cataloging-in-Publication Data

Names: Mattern, Joanne, author.

Title: Cardboard creature challenge! / by Joanne Mattern

Description: Minneapolis, Minnesota : POP!, 2021 | Series: Makerspace cardboard challenge! | Includes online resources and index.

Identifiers: ISBN 9781532167928 (lib. bdg.) | ISBN 9781644944523 (pbk.) | ISBN 9781532169021 (ebook)

Subjects: LCSH: Cardboard art--Juvenile literature. | Crafts (Handicrafts)--Juvenile literature. | Creative thinking in children--Juvenile literature. | Maker spaces--Juvenile literature.

Classification: DDC 745.54--dc23

WELCOME TO DiscoverRoo!

Pop open this book and you'll find QR codes loaded with information, so you can learn even more!

Scan this code* and others like it while you read, or visit the website below to make this book pop!

popbooksonline.com/creature-challenge

*Scanning QR codes requires a web-enabled smart device with a QR code reader app and a camera.

TABLE OF CONTENTS

CHAPTER 1
Adaptations 4

CHAPTER 2
Food and Safety 10

CHAPTER 3
Creature Challenge 16

CHAPTER 4
Improving Your Design 24

Making Connections 30
Glossary 31
Index 32
Online Resources 32

CHAPTER 1
ADAPTATIONS

Earth is home to approximately 8.7 million **species** of animals. Each species lives in a specific **habitat**. Types of habitats include the ocean and the desert. Each species has changed over time to fit its

WATCH A VIDEO HERE!

Tropical rain forests are home to 80 percent of the world's land-based plants and animals.

habitat. These **adaptations** help the

animals survive.

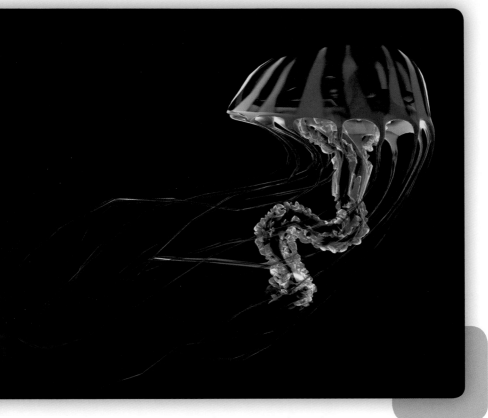

A jellyfish moves by pulling water into its body and then forcing the water out again.

Some adaptations are physical. Each animal's body parts are especially suited to where it lives. For example, a dolphin has flippers and a tail. They help it move through the water.

A mountain goat

has hooves. They

help it climb

mountains.

A duck's webbed feet help it paddle through water.

THINK ABOUT IT

Many animals live in deserts. What adaptations might help animals survive there?

Other adaptations are behavioral.

Some animals have behaviors that help

them survive cold winters. Many birds fly

south. They go to warmer areas. They can

Some octopuses carry around shells to hide inside. This behavior helps the octopuses stay safe.

Leopards will drag their food up a tree to keep it away from other animals that might want to eat it.

find more food there during winter. Bears

use their claws to dig dens. Then they go

into a deep sleep. Bears save energy this

way. They do not have to eat as much

to survive.

CHAPTER 2
FOOD AND SAFETY

Each animal's body is suited to where the animal lives. But it is also suited to what the animal eats. For example, sharp teeth help some animals tear or rip meat. Flat teeth help other animals chew plants.

LEARN MORE HERE!

Birds don't have teeth at all. They swallow their food whole. Or they break food apart with their beaks.

This owl will swallow a whole muskrat at once. Then it will cough up the muskrat's bones, nails, and teeth in a small pellet.

Predators often have eyes that face forward. Their eyes help them hunt other animals. **Prey** often have eyes on the sides of their heads. Their eyes help them see all around them.

With eyes on the sides of its head, an elk has to move its head only slightly to see all the way around itself.

THINK ABOUT IT

How might being able to see all around itself help a prey animal stay safe?

A TIGER'S ADAPTATIONS

stripes on the fur to make it harder to see

large, strong body for catching and killing large prey

eyes at the front of the head to help it judge distances

rough tongue to pull meat from bones while eating

longer back legs for jumping

long claws to grab and hold prey

An anteater's tongue can be up to 2 feet (0.6 m) long.

Predators use specific body parts to help them find their prey. For example, an anteater uses its long tongue to slurp up tiny ants. A woodpecker uses its strong beak to drill into trees. Then it eats the insects found inside the trees.

Some animals use bright colors to warn that they are dangerous to eat.

STAYING SAFE

Some animals' bodies help them avoid predators. Thick shells or sharp spikes make some animals hard to eat. Other animals have poison in their bodies. Predators do not go after these animals as much. Some animals stay safe using **camouflage**. They hide in plain sight. Other animals defend themselves with sharp claws.

CHAPTER 3
CREATURE CHALLENGE

Challenge yourself to make a creature

out of cardboard. You can make an

animal that already exists. Or, you can

invent a new **species**. First, draw your

creature on paper. Think about what

COMPLETE AN ACTIVITY HERE!

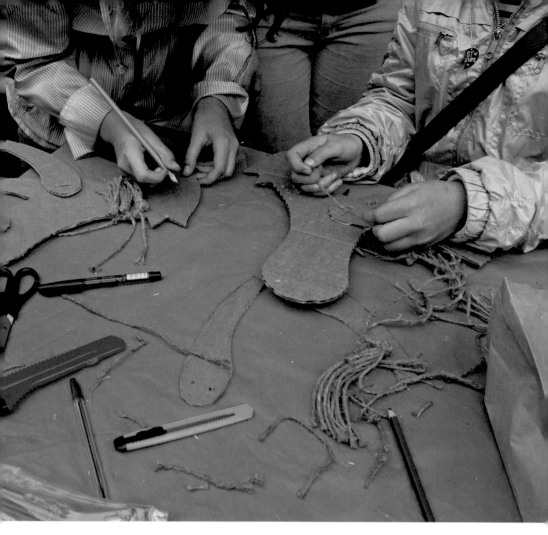

Students make horses out of cardboard. They use string for the manes and tails.

body parts you want it to have. Then,

start building.

This caterpillar is made from an egg carton.

Common animal body parts include

tails, claws, wings, horns, and shells.

What materials could you use to build

these parts? How could you connect the

different parts?

You could cut slits into pieces of cardboard to fit them together.

You could give your creature several ears or eyes.

This cardboard creature has two legs for walking upright.

Some body parts help animals move.

How will your creature move? What body

parts will help it run, climb, or swim?

THINK ABOUT IT

How could you attach your creature's body parts so they can be moved?

The legs of this cardboard creature are attached with paper fasteners.

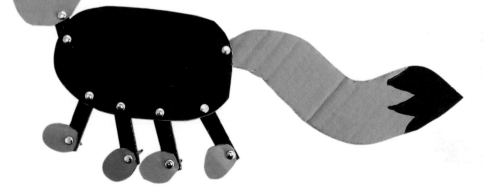

SUPPLY LIST

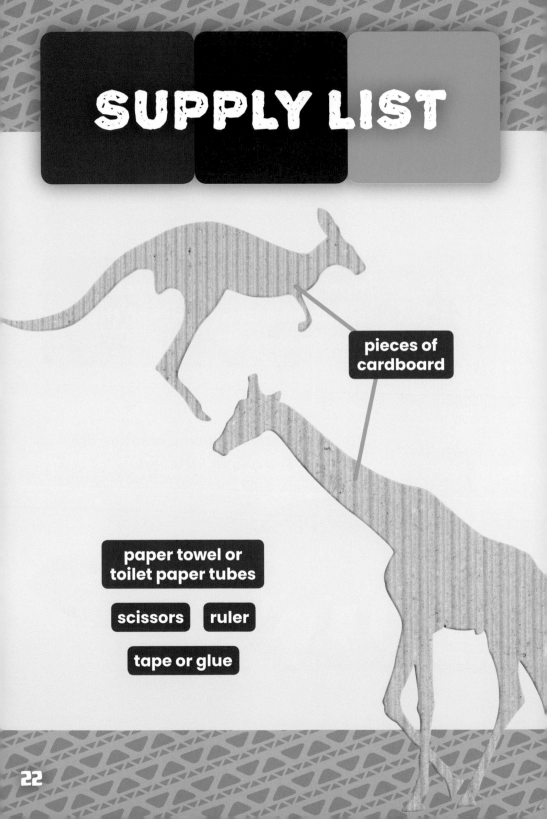

pieces of cardboard

paper towel or toilet paper tubes

scissors   ruler

tape or glue

paint and paintbrushes

rubber bands

crayons or markers **paper clips** **string or yarn**

paper and pencil **pushpins** **paper fasteners**

CHAPTER 4
IMPROVING YOUR DESIGN

Every animal has **adaptations**. They help the animal live in a certain **habitat**. Think about where your creature will live. Is it hot or cold there? Is it wet or dry? What parts could help your creature survive?

LEARN MORE HERE!

The scales on a snake's belly help it grip surfaces such as sand or rock and push itself forward.

This cardboard creature could use its two large pincers to fight off a predator.

Animals face many dangers in their habitats. Some animals fight back against **predators**. Other animals run and hide. How will your creature respond to danger? What body parts will help it respond in this way?

This cardboard animal could use its large mouth to swallow attackers.

This cardboard bird's green coloring could help it hide in a forest.

Many animals use their coloring

to stay safe. Think about what color

you want your creature to be. Will your

creature be all one color? Will it have

stripes or spots?

These girls are using paint to color their cardboard creatures.

THINK ABOUT IT

How could you color your creature to help it stay safe in its habitat?

MAKING CONNECTIONS

TEXT-TO-SELF

Do you or your friends have pets? How do each pet's body parts help it eat, move, or stay safe?

TEXT-TO-TEXT

Have you read other books about animal adaptations? What did you learn?

TEXT-TO-WORLD

Many adaptations help animals find food or stay safe. Which do you think is more important?

GLOSSARY

adaptation – a trait that helps an animal survive in its environment.

camouflage – a pattern, color, or shape that helps an animal blend in with its surroundings.

habitat – the area where an animal normally lives.

predator – an animal that hunts other animals for food.

prey – an animal that is hunted by other animals.

species – a group of animals or plants of the same kind that can reproduce.

INDEX

adaptations, 5–8, 24

body parts, 6, 14, 17–18, 21, 27

camouflage, 15

eyes, 12–13

food, 9, 11

habitats, 4–5, 24, 26, 29

predators, 12, 14–15, 26

prey, 12–14

safety, 12, 15, 28–29

teeth, 10–11

ONLINE RESOURCES
popbooksonline.com

Scan this code* and others like it while you read, or visit the website below to make this book pop!

popbooksonline.com/creature-challenge

*Scanning QR codes requires a web-enabled smart device with a QR code reader app and a camera.